Love & Bliss

Other Books by Yogi Amrit Desai

Kripalu Yoga: Meditation in Motion, Books I and II

Working Miracles of Love

Happiness is Now

*Amrit Yoga: Explore, Expand and Experience
the Spiritual Depth of Yoga*

A Yogic Perspective on the 12 Steps

Amrit Yoga and The Yoga Sutras

Love & Bliss

Meditations on the Art of Living

YOGI AMRIT DESAI

Red Elixir | Rhinebeck, NY   Yoga Network International | Salt Springs, FL

Published by Yoga Network International, Inc.
PO Box 5340
Salt Springs, FL 32134

www.amritkala.com

in co-operation with
Red Elixir
27 Lamoree Road
Rhinebeck, NY 12572

ISBN 978-0-9719455-3-1

Library of Congress Control Number: 2010923333

Table of Contents

Meditations on the Art of Living
Introduction
By Lila Ivey, editor

The search for happiness is universal and usually unsuccessful. Most of our assets, skills and knowledge are invested in finding that something that will bring us true and lasting peace, joy and satisfaction. Happiness is perceived as a destination—once we arrive, we will have more power, more prosperity, more recognition, and more acceptance. We spend our entire life in this pursuit, yet how many of us can say that we are truly fulfilled or happy with what we have achieved?

For thousands of years, the message of yoga has been that lasting happiness is indeed attainable. It is not elusive—it is our natural state and is available to everyone, not just an enlightened few. The great yogis discovered it in an entirely different way than those whose pursuit is driven by what they can control in the external world of possessions and power. The great yogic traditions teach us that happiness is not derived from what you have, but who you are. Yoga does not seek a happiness that is temporal and fleeting. Yoga seeks the supreme happiness of ecstasy, an enduring fulfillment that comes through unity of body, mind, heart and spirit.

The meditations in this book, derived from the collected writings of Yogi Amrit Desai, explore four principles essential to accessing this supreme bliss. They have been carefully transcribed with awareness of the potential loss of depth involved when editing the words of a master. Particular attention has been paid to preserving the specific wording only clarifying the language when it interfered with rather than enhanced the meaning. Read deeply into the meaning rather than into the words themselves—the significance of the meditations is most often revealed in the silence between the lines. The subjects themselves are elusive and sometimes contradictory by their very nature, which reflect the paradoxical unity of yoga itself.

The writings that have emerged from these basic precepts of yogic teaching are just as elusive and may appear cryptic. Most are written in free verse, an open form of poetry. Read and re-read these passages. Sit with them. Feel them. Experience them. Allow their message to unfold, remembering that poetry, especially spiritual poetry, exists beyond the words. This is a book that must be read not with your mind but with your heart.

Another great teacher, Bhagwan Shree Rajneesh, once said

> *Poetry is more music, less language.*
> *It is more a feeling and less a thought.*
> *It eludes and that is the beauty of it …*
> *It is like a river moving, not like a pond.*
> *Prose is a pond; poetry is a river*
> *The truth is not that which is written,*
> *The truth is that which is hidden.*

The meditations flow from four basic yogic concepts that provide us with the opportunity to experience happiness in everything we do:

1. *Remaining the Witness*
2. *Living in the Present*
3. *Loving Unconditionally*
4. *Moving from Becoming to Being*

I. Remaining the Witness

Without realizing it, we live in a state of constant judgment. Our mind instantly makes a judgment about everything that happens to us—either it is good or bad, right or wrong. We give ourselves the role of the judge.

This judge is subjective—not objective. The judge doesn't experience his experience. Rather he experiences the *interpretation* of his experience. The judge cannot directly experience impersonal reality in the presence of his personal judgment, so he invariably misses what is present.

The perceived object itself has no inherent power. It is the judge who assigns power to the object. This is why we say, "Beauty is in the eye of the beholder." So is ugliness. Happiness is in the heart of the perceiver. So is unhappiness. Every experience is charged, conditioned and distorted by our personalized perception.

Therefore whatever appears to come from the objective world is subjective perception. Anger, blame, shame, guilt and fear are only perceptions of our experiences. They have no objective reality. Every interpretation of good or bad, right or wrong, success or failure, happiness or unhappiness, is an implanted experience that has no basis in reality. Every perception we create is a personalized experience of reality, which is universally impersonal. This is why we often feel so cheated by life...because we insist that things should be as we want them to be, not the way they are.

The way to remove yourself from judging is through the medium of witness, the dispassionate observer. The Witness has no conditions to sensations of pleasure or pain, comfort or discomfort. There is no liking or disliking. By being the Witness, you learn to *experience the experience* rather than distort the experience with your preprogrammed concepts. When you feel with equanimity, you are simultaneously embracing opposites. You begin to live in the reality of complementary polarity, rather than in the self-created world of duality, which separates opposites, labeling them as good and bad.

To move from personal perception to impersonal reality, you must fire the judge and hire the Witness.

II. Living in the Present

Remaining in the present...between the past and the future...is living in the narrow space of the Now. This very moment is the only one that matters. It is beyond time/space boundaries. The present moment is eternal. It is what is before us and holds the potential of all possibilities.

Christ was referring to the concept of living in the present when he said, "It is easier for a camel to pass through the eye of a needle than for a rich man to enter the gate of heaven." Christ had nothing against people of wealth or of prosperity, but he knew that the rich man carries the burdens of the past and expectations of the future, and that even the gate of heaven is not wide enough for him to pass through carrying so much baggage. The camel, on the other hand, bears no such burdens. It is a simple beast with no agendas. Living in the present means that you hold on to neither memories of the past nor dreams of the future. You are simply here...now.

When we live in the past, our perceptions are of unresolved events. What do we do when a current event reminds us of a past event? We react.

"Reaction" means we unconsciously reactivate past experiences and mistake them for the present. It filters our present and re-shapes it according to our preprogrammed, unconscious memories of the past. When we ignore what is occurring in the present, we are driven by unconsciousness. Our reactions show up as either addiction or fear. A perception, conditioned by our personal reaction, is the womb where all self-caused suffering is conceived.

Reaction is from the past; response is in the present.

Reaction is mechanical; response is deliberate.

Reaction is unconscious; response is conscious.

When we live in the future, we create a false world. It exists only in our mind. Excessively engaged and anxious about the future outcome to our dreams, we fail to see, feel or experience what is already present. Greed thrives on the future and carries with it a sense of insecurity. Even when dreams and desires are fulfilled, the sense of insecurity and insufficiency that goes with it eclipses the outcome. Desires are insatiable. They consume our success, create new desires and leave us perpetually hungry for more.

To be in the present you must let go of the burdens of the past as well as solving problems in the future. The present is the sacred shrine of the divine. The future cannot survive in the present, nor can the past. The present is omnipresent. It is all encompassing. It is all there is. It has no beginning. It has no end. It has no past or future. It is whole.

When you live partially in the past and partially in the future, you are divided. Thus separated, you cannot enter the shrine of the divine that exists only in the present. However, when you are total and undivided, you are instantly here.

This is the state of embodying the spirit where your body is disclaimed by your ego-mind and reclaimed by the spirit. Your body becomes the holy temple for the being that you are manifesting in the here and now.

III. Loving Unconditionally

Love is not romance. It is not emotion. It is not attachment to another. It is not a satisfying sexual experience. It is none of the things we so commonly associate it with in our culture.

Love is love only when it is unconditional. Any condition you place on love is actually fear in disguise. Conditions represent distrust in the power of love. What you ask from or expect from another creates an invisible wall of separation. The love you want from others can only come from within. It disappears when you ask for it and reappears when are you willing to give it. When all doing disappears, your total undivided presence is the fulfillment of your inborn evolutionary urge to merge. Learning to love with complete acceptance and openness, allowing the other to show up however he or she is in that moment, without any change whatsoever, is an expression of unconditional love.

Only when I allow you to be you,
Do I allow me to be me.

The deepest experience of love is union, where the walls of separation collapse and two melt into one—then yoga happens, whether it is in yoga practice, in your work or in any of your relationships.

IV. Moving from Becoming to Being

When your focus is outward-bound, your center is outside of yourself. Your search for power is externalized. When you focus inward, you connect with the source of power within.

If you are driven by insecurity and deficiency, every one of your activities, including the practice of yoga, is outward-bound. This alienation from your own inner source of power attempts to prove its worth by achieving recognition, acceptance, respect and love. That is its central motivation. All your expressions must have demonstrable accomplishments that would earn love and respect from others.

Those who are driven by "deficiency" consciousness live on the superficial circumference of life where they have no connection to the source within. Everything they do is an attempt to find their center somewhere other than inside themselves. This is not to disparage those who win awards, break world records and excel in art, business or sports. But, in the end, many over-achievers are left with a feeling of emptiness and loneliness—a void that no accomplishment can fill. What then?

Regardless of how resourceful you are, how many skills you have, or how efficient you are, if you are driven by "deficiency" consciousness, you cannot solve any real problems in your life. People who seek recognition and power outside do not hesitate to sacrifice their own health, peace of mind, or their friends and loved ones, in their attempt to solve problems that do not exist. In reality, you are both your worst enemy and your best friend. When you are caught in outward-bound activities, you tend to create hell within in order to create heaven without. Again, the teachings of Christ speak to us as clearly today as they did 2,000 years ago about the situations we create for ourselves: "Seek ye the kingdom of heaven within."

The practice of yoga is about shifting from becoming, achieving or accomplishing to being what we truly are. It is returning from externalized motivation to connecting with the infinite source of power within. It is the process of getting away from outward-bound activities and moving toward the inwardly focused self-sourcing way of thinking, feeling, acting and doing.

Amrit Yoga: Union of body, mind, heart and spirit

The approach to yoga developed by Yogi Amrit Desai over the last 40 years provides specific techniques, tools and principles that help you move towards the source within. It uses the body as an entry point. The physical discipline deals with the body; the mental discipline with the mind; the discipline of love with the heart. The spiritual dimension of yoga deals with the integration of body, mind, heart and soul, the totality of which is your Being.

These are the extensions through which our being expresses and manifests. Regardless of which extension (body, mind or heart) is predominantly engaged, the other two must remain actively engaged in co-creative process for the being (soul) to bloom.

You cannot enter the dimension of yoga, the integrated state of being, by engaging in only one limb of Patanjali's eight-limbed system of yoga. When one faculty is exclusively engaged, such as the body-centered approach in the practice of Hatha Yoga, and other faculties of our being, such as the mind and heart, are not deliberately brought into an active co-creative role, there is no harmonious integration of the whole being. When we are practicing physical yoga and our mind is off shopping or picking up the children, this creates conflict. If there is no joy in the practice and it feels like drudgery, then we are in conflict on three levels. We are not practicing yoga—we are practicing conflict.

Using the body as an entry point to the deeper practice of yoga harnesses and harmonizes the mental and emotional bodies. Through meditative awareness (the Witness) and using your bodily sensations as your point of concentration, you focus on the released energy in the repose—the second half of the posture.

From this place of active co-creation—from dynamic postures followed by deeply engaging silences—you enter the integrated state of ecstatic being where body, mind and heart are harmoniously engaged and absorbed in the state of oneness—yoga. This harmony is the state of being an undivided presence.

The core practice that integrates all the extensions of our being is inwardly focused, mindful, meditative awareness. Meditation and concentration are a necessary part of the practice. Entering the spiritual dimension of integrative awareness heals not only the physical body, but the mental and emotional bodies as well.

When you shift to an inward-bound focus, all your activities become directed toward connecting to the infinite source of power, creativity, strength and endurance within. As you move from becoming to being, problems you perceive as coming from outside are, in fact, coming from within. You learn to take complete responsibility, which in turn, completely changes the way you experience and interpret your life. You no longer live with shame or blame as an escape. Your have the ability to choose your own response instead of being the victim of your own unconscious reactions. You begin to experience freedom from dependency and demands on others, which gives you a sense of self-sourcing and self-empowerment.

Integrative awareness dissolves duality and melts into divine unity, where the doer disappears into doing—the actor becomes the action—the performer merges into the performance. This approach takes your yoga practice from doing to becoming to being.

Part 1
Remaining the Witness

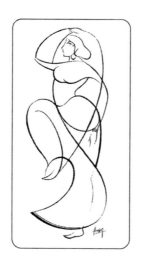

The journey of transformation
begins with inward focus.
Meditative awareness harmonizes
unconscious forces,
the restless mind
and emotional conflicts.

Mindful meditative awareness transports you to another dimension
where you experience the unifying power of the spirit.
It leads you to a sacred space in the cave of your heart,
where you can return again and again
to regain the protective power of the divine that is always present within you.

As you enter this sacred space,
leave your ego-mind outside and invite the Witness inside.

The Witness is like a black hole.

Whatever you bring to it
disappears into the void of nothingness,
leaving nothing for you to do.

The most beautiful part of the witness
is that you have no obligation to
process anything,
control anything or
expect anything.

Simply be in it.

Every soul is charged with an evolutionary mission
to realize its inborn divine potential.
Life is a perpetual therapeutic irritation.
It provides a compelling force to drive you toward the completion of your mission.

When you deny a painful experience,
it goes underground as a pending debt of unfinished karma.
When you block pain,
you may feel temporary relief,
but your karmic account is not closed.

The collection agency will present the lesson again and again
in various forms through apparently unrelated events.
Every event that is not faced fully and consciously comes back
as irritation, emotion, resistance or denial.

Habitual ways of reacting and reliving the same event
perpetuate unconsciousness.
All lessons will be repeated until they are learned.
The debt of karma is paid in consciousness.

Every reaction is the dynamic impact of past karma.

If you cannot stop your reaction, delay it.

If you cannot delay your reaction, divert your attention.

Most importantly, do not react to your first reaction.

Your first reaction is your past karma reappearing in the present.

The second reaction is your choice in the present.

The impact of your karma is judged not by the past,

but how you interact with it in the present.

Emotionally charged reactions
are reflections of the law of karma,
where both free will and fate are in intimate interplay.

Fate is the consequence we experience
from the seeds of karma planted in the past.

Free will provides us with an opening to redesign our future
through consciously living the consequences of past karma in the present.

*All reactions are the direct result
of the unresolved past.*

A hurtful experience is not necessarily the result of bad karma.
It is your perception of it, which makes it either good or bad.
This is your choice.
If you choose to use that experience to evolve to a higher level,
This is your opportunity to be released from old karma.

As Christ was vilified, humiliated and ultimately crucified,
his suffering could have been viewed as very bad karma.
But Christ's suffering was not the result of bad karma.
He did not perceive this experience as failure or as punishment.

Christ did not call on his disciples to take revenge on those who crucified him.
Instead he said, "Forgive them, Father, for they know not what they do."
In the midst of extreme injustice, his interpretation transformed the entire event.
What Christ demonstrated from the cross was the highest lesson he ever taught.
Christ was not born when he was baptized—he was born on the cross.
This is when Jesus became Christ.

The result of karma is not the event that takes place.
It is how you perceive it.
It is not the appearance of pain in the external world that counts.
Your internal interpretation is the real outcome of your karma.

Life comes to you through you,
as you are with yourself.
If you are angry and revengeful or satisfied and happy,
whichever way you are,
that becomes the experience of your life.

It is not about what you have, it is about who you are.
You do not have to work hard to get anywhere,
or to prove anything.

There is no difference between having much or having little.
Internally, your experience of life is not defined by what you have achieved,
but by how you feel about yourself.

When you feel hurt, rejected or frustrated,
the witness of equanimity allows you to embrace the experience
without the reaction of fight or flight.

Choiceless awareness releases you from your preprogrammed perceptions.
It prohibits you from clinging to the past.
It prevents you from escaping into the future.
It allows you to reenter the sacred present.

The Witness creates an opening
for you to embrace opposites without fear or attachment.
The only way to be free from fear is to let go of attachment.
The only way to be free from attachment is to let go of fear.

Embracing opposites means embracing whichever end of the opposite
is present for you at any given time.

Sadhana is inner work.
It is not about changing others.
It is about changing yourself.

When you perceive conflict anywhere in your life,
it is representative of the conflict that lives within you.
When you see that the source of all conflicts and all solutions is inside,
then you take complete responsibility for all your life experiences.

Every adversity is then converted into an asset for transformation.
This self-empowerment is the fruit of sadhana.

Use everything in your life as sadhana.

All of life's interactions are reflections of yourself.
They are designed by universal law to reveal your reactions.
This awareness is possible only when you recognize
that anyone or any situation can trigger a reaction,
emotionally, mentally or physically.

Understand that no one has the power to create that reaction.
No one can push your button unless you already have one.
If you have a karma button, life will arrange itself in such a way
that you will unconsciously invite someone to push it
so you can hold another responsible for your own unhappiness.

True sadhana is when you take responsibility for your karmic button,
rather than blaming the button pusher.
When your intention is to eliminate the button rather than the button pusher,
only then does sadhana begin.

Attachment is fear in disguise.

Attachment and fear are not different things.
They are different names for the same thing.
When you let go of one, the other goes with it.

Fear is that which separates us from our Source.
Fear is what keeps us from getting in touch
with the unlimited source of power and fulfillment that is always present.

When you receive from within
what you have been trying to attain from without,
attachment disappears and fear vanishes.

When you take a stand either for or against what is present,
you are separated from the transcendent timeless now.
When you stand for or against,
you have abandoned the present.
When your fulfillment lies separated from here and now,
it lives in the memory of the past or in the anticipation of the future.
You stand in conflict with what is present.

When you live in the now, there is no room to stand for or against.
You, who is held captive by your personal choice,
must dissolve separation through choiceless awareness.
This opens the door to the state of witness consciousness
that exists only in the present moment.

Witness is the life and breath of the spirit.
The present moment is the presence of the divine
manifesting in the unity of space and time,
subject and object,
lover and the beloved,
the soul and God.

Every spiritual discipline is designed to induce irritation.
The intention is to encounter irritation consciously
rather than react to it habitually.

When you deliberately remove all that you have been hiding behind,
You begin to encounter irritations as the Witness.
You become the dispassionate observer.
You are now the one who does not bury, deny or suppress
everything that has been preventing your spiritual evolution.

Just as debris that has settled to the bottom of the pond
must be stirred up before it can be cleared,
the practice of spiritual discipline is designed to agitate sleeping irritations
and bring them to the surface.

Although it may seem contrary to what you eventually want,
this is the process a spiritual aspirant must go through.
You cannot clear the debris that is holding you back
without first stirring it up.

Life naturally provides opportunities
to encounter everything you have been avoiding.

When you face pain, discomfort or insult, you reach a point of toleration.
Irritation and resistance are programmed into your unconscious.
This is your opportunity to convert
habitual negative reaction into conscious deliberate response.

If you resist your toleration point,
the unconscious instinct sees only two possibilities:
fight or flight.

There is a third possibility.
You can choose to encounter the experience consciously,
where you are neither fighting nor fleeing.
This is the Witness.

By entering the witness state, you create a new way
to experience the same situation without irritation or reaction.
This is where mechanical reaction is transformed into consciousness,
allowing you to explore new dimensions of true empowerment and fulfillment.

Discipline means that each time you reach a toleration point in your life,
you use it as an opportunity to move beyond it.

Welcome your point of toleration.

Be grateful for the possibilities it offers.

It holds the potential to release you from the inhibitions of old patterns.

If you resist it,

your turn it into the battlefield of fight or flight.

If you encounter it consciously,

you turn resistance into transformation.

When the challenges of life
bring you to your toleration point,
you have arrived at a crossroad where either ego appears
or the Witness happens.

This is the frontier where you choose fight or flight,
or you embrace the experience where there is neither fight nor flight.

This window of opening is willingness to face what is, as it is.
It is entering the experience unconditionally,
feeling all that is present without judgment, interpretation,
guilt, shame or blame.
This is the point of tapas, the spiritual fire that burns everything you have been
preserving as yourself.

This is a painful journey.
It means giving up all that you have adopted to protect your self-image,
which lives under the protection of unconscious instincts.

As the mask of the ego burns, the Self is revealed.
The Witness neutralizes the power struggle between the self-image and the Self.
The Witness reveals the all-encompassing nature of the Self,
which absorbs the conflicting forces of duality,
taking them to the other side and
transforming them into the integrated force of unity and ecstasy.

Our thoughts are waves on the ocean of consciousness.

Waves emerge from the ocean and merge back into the ocean.
The form of a wave changes,
but oceanic consciousness remains changeless.

Consciousness manifests through a multiplicity of forms,
but consciousness itself remains formless.

How do you manage the unconscious behavior
that invades everything you do—
from performing yoga postures
to driving your car
to relating to your loved ones?
To do this, you must be the Witness of your own reaction.

Reaction is always caused by pain and fear.
It can be physical, mental or emotional.
Our natural instinct is to enter the fight or flight reflex.
We either try to change what is happening
or move away from what we believe is causing the pain.

Observe your reactions with neither fight nor flight.
Remain in the experience without attaching personal likes or dislikes.
Strive for the absence of internal reactions.
Be present for however life manifests.

The state of Witness happens

only when you are willing to bypass
your personal choices that are conditioned by fears or addictions.
You live in a "separative" consciousness
that is actively divided by your attractions and repulsions.
The transcendental state of unity consciousness
rises above the duality of opposites.

Regardless of the experience,
learn to embrace it unconditionally.
In the absence of personal choice,
become open to the direct experience of universal reality.
By making the choice to be sensitive to your experience as it truly is,
you open the door, embracing your life unconditionally.

When you live in the Witness,

you expose yourself to both pleasure and pain.
Pleasure and pain enter through the same door.
When you close the door to pain,
you also close it to pleasure.

To keep the door open, be in choiceless awareness.
In the absence of judgment, the silent Witness is the opening
for an increased range of feeling.
The Witness has no conditions to sensations of pleasure or pain,
comfort or discomfort.
There is no liking or disliking.
In the presence of choiceless awareness,
you increase your capacity to feel more of everything.

When you allow yourself to feel all sensations,
your ability to embrace opposites is simultaneously increased.
This is the experience of unity among apparent duality.

Life is not separate from death.
Breath in is not separate from breath out.
Expansion is not separate from contraction.
Tension is not separate from relaxation.

What we call "our life"
is the product of complementary polarity,
the seat of underlying unity.
The opposites of birth and death, breath in and breath out,
are the essence of life-sustaining polarity.

The body voices its needs through
comfort and discomfort,
pleasure and pain,
hunger and fulfillment.

When we choose one over the other,
we create conflicting duality out of complementary polarity.
The Witness allows us to emerge from the compelling force of
addiction to pleasure and fear of pain
and return to the nurturing power of unity through polarity.

In selecting one pole of polarity and dismissing the other,
We create duality.

Duality is man-made.

It is a destructive force.

Duality is a personal distortion of the all-pervading creative presence of polarity.

Our life is part of the universal unity of polarity.

When we choose one pole over the other,

success over failure,

happiness over unhappiness or

pleasure over pain,

we become the recipient of the duality we have created through choice.

As the intensity grows from choice to attraction

Attraction to attachment,

attachment to passion,

passion to addiction,

addiction to obsession,

the degree of blindness to reality grows exponentially.

This blindness forces us to ignore one thing to get something else.

It is selective memory to get what we want.

It is distorted reasoning to avoid what we are afraid of.

Fear-based ignoring is the true meaning of "ignorance."

As we let go of our attraction and repulsion,

increased integration gives birth to wisdom from within.

We then see reality as it is, without the need to grab or avoid.

It opens us to all-embracing, unconditional love and compassion.

Polarity is at the core of our entire existence.
It is at the core of creation, evolution and the sustenance of life.
Opposing poles play a crucial role in carrying out all life-giving processes.
These apparent opposites cannot exist independent of each other.

When this polarity enters the separative human consciousness
that chooses one against the other,
the psyche of the one who creates the separation
suffers from self-created duality.

Unity manifests as a paradox
where the beginning is not separate from the end,
where breathing in is not separate from breathing out,
where success is not separate from failure,
and where life is not separate from death.

The Witness produces paradoxical unity
where opposites are present simultaneously,
existing in harmony and oneness.
In Witness, you embrace opposites with equanimity.

Reality holds that there are opposite poles
to every part of the cosmos.
While they appear to be separate,
they are complementary in relationship, creating the whole.
Each exists because of the other.

The symbol of yin and yang illustrates polarity in black and white.
Together yin and yang form a complete circle,
They nest in perfect synchronicity.
A speck of each enveloped by the other.
This is unity in polarity.

Duality is human and personal.
Polarity is universal and impersonal.
Duality is the cause of all human suffering.
Polarity is the source of all healing and harmony.

When you evaluate who you are in terms of relativity,
no matter how much better you get, you are only relatively better.
All that is perceived through relativity
is meaningful for sustaining life in the external world
But it is disruptive to the spirit, which only reveals itself in unity.

The mind that operates in duality creates a personal world of illusive relativity.
It cannot work in the field of universal reality of oneness that we are.
Unity cannot be recognized in terms of either relativity or duality.

The body-mind understands everything in relative terms.
The Witness operates from beyond the body-mind.
It transcends relativity.

All illusions are created in duality and are resolved in unity.
This is the paradigm shift from disruptive duality
to the sacred dimension of union.

Cause and effect seem separate,
but they are not two systems.
Cause is connected to effect through time.
Cause uses time to eventually manifest as effect,
Cause is inextricably bound to effect through time and space.
Together, they form karma—cause is the seed, effect is the result.

The one who remains untouched by either cause or effect
exists beyond beginning and end.
Witness is beyond. It is alpha and omega—it is time-transcendent.

Witness is timeless;
it does not belong to the duality dimension of cause and effect.
It is beyond duality, relativity, time, space and mind.
There is no karma in the dimension of unity.

Witness is the omnipresent, omnipotent, omniscient dimension of our being,
our soul, that is the presence of God within us.

Witness generates the fire that burns karma.
It is non-participative choiceless awareness,
where the observer does not judge, evaluate or analyze.
It allows the object of awareness to be as it is.
The Witness remains the changeless observer of all changing objects.
The observer does not interfere with what is, by imposing personal choice for or
against what is present.
This is the surrender of personal will to impersonal reality.
It is the meaning of Christ's teaching: "My Lord, thy will be done, not mine."

Night and day are one.
When seen through time, they appear separate.
Yet you will never see the dawn if you are afraid to go through the night.

Cause and effect are one.
When seen through the eyes of fear, they appear separate.
You will never realize the cause if you do not embrace the effect.

Success and failure, pleasure and pain,
health and sickness, birth and death are not separate.
They are complementary expressions of the system of life,
Co-existing as one.

If we separate one from the other,
it does not change the law of polarity.
The human attempt to divide unity turns polarity into duality,
manifesting as fear and addiction.

Duality is separation from the Source.
Polarity is connection to the Source.
When you embrace polarity, you choose unity.

Unity begins with the recognition
that I am the source of all my problems and of all my solutions.

Duality sees the solution to life's problems as being outside of oneself.
Searching for solutions externally is compensation for what we imagine is missing from our lives.

Duality is a split from oneness; it is a separation from God.
Duality is the world of relativity.
Only the ego-mind and the body can participate in that world.
It is limited by time and space.

In duality, there is destructive illusory relativity.
In polarity, there is life-enhancing relativity.
In the experience of oneness,
there is no room for the duality of the mind or the senses to enter.

When we recognize that we are already complete,
we can simultaneously live in the world and the spirit.
From this vantage point, we live in unity in the midst of diversity.

Giving silent voice to the Witness
quiets the noise of conflict.

The Witness holds no judgments,

makes no demands and offers no opinions.

The Witness simply is—total and undivided.

Integrative awareness is a potent tool.

It unites the conflicting voices of our self-image.

Through intention and commitment,

Witness consciousness brings conflicting polarity into co-creative unity.

When the voices of the self-image are silenced,

you begin to listen to your own true voice, the voice of your Self.

Integrated, you move out of the conflicting forces of the lower three centers of

survival, sensation and power,

and step into the heart and the higher centers of love and compassion.

Integrative awareness keeps you present, total and undivided,

regardless of what you do or where you go.

The silent Witness stands apart, but it is not mute.
As you give voice to your Witness,
the wisdom of unity consciousness begins to emerge
in the midst of conflicting duality.

The voice of the Witness whispers:
"I observe my body resisting and my mind reacting.
But I am not my body, my mind or my reactions.

I have a body, a mind and reactions, but they are not 'me.'
I have the power to distance myself from what I observe.
I am an observer of what my body and mind are doing.
I observe my body-mind — fighting, rationalizing, justifying, escaping.

I am a non-participating witness to the reactive body-mind.
As a result, I remain above all that I observe.
In the Witness, I diffuse the power of my self-image,
And enable myself to return to the Source again and again."

Conflict in relationships is inevitable.

It is an externalization of internal conflict.

All karmic seeds represent our unresolved relationships.

Holding karma is a split from reality.

When we try to resolve relationships by controlling outside forces,

we merely extend that incompleteness.

Internal separation will reveal itself in any relationship

we establish outside ourselves.

This awareness is an opportunity to use conflict

as a vehicle for completion and wholeness.

Separation is born of unconsciousness.
It is supported by a large army.
Its soldiers are fear, competition and jealousy.

Unity consciousness is alone.
It exists without an army,
yet it has infinite power that no force can conquer.

When you operate from separative consciousness,
one part is always at war with the remaining part.
Division can never be as powerful as the whole.
Even when you fight for union,
you only reinforce division.

Duality cannot win; it can only further divide.
Unity does not fight and therefore remains whole.
Wars fought for peace invariably plant the seeds of separation,
reinforcing the conflict they were trying to heal.

What is accomplished in peace
can never be accomplished through war.
What is accomplished in relaxation
cannot be accomplished through tension.

Letting go naturally attains what can never be achieved by tension.
That which can never be attained by war is achieved by being at peace.

Just as you cannot enter a war for peace,
you cannot enter stress to be relaxed.

When you struggle to overcome the boundaries you encounter,
it is as futile as fighting a war for peace.

Pain is not punishment. It is a message of healing.

Pain is not torment for sins committed, but an opportunity for growth.

Resisting pain reduces attention to pure sensation.

In resistance, you will miss the message.

Living in pain consciously eventually releases you from it.

When you go to the very core of pain,

you will discover the secrets of pleasure.

Pleasure and pain are complementary.

They are two poles connected by the same ladder.

The ladder that brings you down is the same ladder that takes you up.

That which brings pleasure also brings pain.

That which brings pain is also a conduit to pleasure.

Pain is an opportunity to return to physical, mental and emotional health.

In moments of deep emotional reaction,

be present and embrace the experience.

God does not deliver pain.

God delivers life.

Whatever you see with attention, you feel.
Whatever you hear with attention, you feel.
Whatever you touch, taste or smell with attention, you feel.

You connect with the world through the five physical senses.
When the body is blocked with stress or your attention is distracted,
energy is fragmented and your ability to feel is diminished.

Stress cuts you off from your heart.
It draws energy into your head.
When you let go of self-destructive thoughts,
energy is disengaged from the head and flows to the heart.

When the heart is open, your body is relaxed.
Your attention is free and focused.
Once again, you regain your ability to truly feel.

Feeling comes through the medium of the body
and the heart.
Feelings come through the medium of the mind.

Feeling is pure sensation.
Feelings are emotional reactions.

Feelings arise from self-concepts, fears, personal biases and belief systems.
They are a distortion of the pure sensation of feeling.

Pure sensation is freedom from feelings.

Your heart and your body represent your feeling center.
The mind represents the thinking center.
It filters perceptions through personal attraction and repulsion.
It has the power to overshadow the feeling center.

All labels of pleasure and pain,
comfort and discomfort,
likes and dislikes,
are personal values.
They prevent you from being in the purity of the feeling center.

When the mind merges into the silent Witness,
your feeling center is unconditionally open to receive.
Anchored fully in your feeling center,
you are present to enter the experience as it is, without labels.

To open your heart, remain a non-participative, choiceless witness to all
that you hear,
that you see,
that you feel.

We continue doing the same things...

Always expecting different results.

Your self-image is an acquired social mask.

It is the false persona you present to the world.

There is no need to protect it.

In reality, you cannot lose what you never had.

After you let go of what you have acquired,

what is left is who you really are.

What survives is the Self.

We have an animal body, a human mind
and a divine potential.

The involuntary functions and instinctive urges of the animal body
operate in harmonious interaction to sustain life.

The human mind has the power
to intervene with the biological urges of the animal body.
It has the freedom to go against natural urges or to act in harmony with them.
It is an evolutionary gift.

The mind also has the potential to transcend the limitations of the instinctual
dimension through which the body-mind operates.
This is the ultimate spiritual attainment.
This is our divine potential.

The single cause of stress is unconsciousness.
Unconscious forces hijack your ability to choose your own response.
They prevent you from managing your life deliberately and consciously.
Unconsciousness reacts to what it perceives.
Consciousness responds to what is present.

Consciousness answers without distortion from the reactivated past.
The past has no relationship with the present.
Remaining the Witness is the means to regaining your lost sense of responsibility.

Conscious awareness empowers you to choose responses
that are in harmony with your health and higher centers.

The silent Witness exists in the domain of grace.
In that dimension, every object of your awareness
provides the facility to disassociate from identification with that object.
This is disassociation from your self-image,
self-concepts, belief systems, personal biases and fears.

Once you have established yourself on the seat of the soul,
you learn the art of disassociating from all of your past.
You abandon unconscious reactions to patterns shaped by painful experiences.

When you remain a silent observer to all that you encounter,
either in the practice of yoga postures or the psychic postures life puts you in,
you enter the domain of grace.

Choiceless awareness is a self-correcting tool of
the divine force.
It automatically augments that which is for you
and removes that which is against you.
When you are the Witness, your ego need not be the judge.
You neither blame others nor yourself for your unhappiness.
The Witness prevents toxic emotions that fuel the fires of judgment.
Entry into the dimension of grace
comes through renouncing both shame and blame.

Remain a silent observer.
Let the feeling be processed.
Learn to feel pain and disappointment,
without letting your ego-mind analyze
who did it,
why did they do it,
why didn't you stop it,
why didn't you act differently or
how you can now change the other so they don't repeat the act.
All such questions are out of the question.

Witness is a new way of solving problems
where you do absolutely nothing to solve them.
There is only the non-participative choiceless Witness,
watching the parade of all objects of awareness,
observing thoughts, emotions, reactions, fears, sensations and opinions.

Eventually, a dispassionate distance emerges,
separating what you perceive to be yourself from the Self of your soul.

Performing all actions with meditative, mindful awareness,

one passes from...

personality to the impersonal essence of being,

from dichotomy to harmony,

from duality to unity.

Remain a distant observer of feelings, sensations, pain, pleasure and thoughts.

Take a sustained look at whatever is happening,

with no reactions arising from the body or the mind.

Place no judgment or labels on the objects of your perception.

Allow the essence to grow and the persona to diminish.

Trust in the essence of your being.

It is self-regulating and self-luminous.

You do not have to do anything to avoid wrong or attract goodness.

Trust your being completely with no effort and no doubt.

No muscle in your body tenses, your eyes and face remain soft.

Let all doing pass by.

Watch as your self-image loses its grip, clinging to survival.

The Witness wins and fear loses.

Your shakti rises to higher centers.

Allow the growing essence to evolve in the womb of faith, patience and love.

You have complete freedom to choose what you do.
You have no freedom to choose the results of what you do.
If you value the results for what they are,
they become Prasad*.

Prasad – sweet food given in love by the master to his disciple.

Part II
Living in the Present

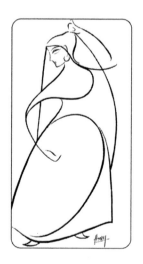

Life is a journey without a destination.
It is an infinite unfolding process.

Any destination you plan is the extension of your imagination.
Obsessing over your arrival creates impatience and anticipation.

When you live here, but anticipate a future out there,
you become divided between here and there.
The greater the attachment to the dream,
the more you are drawn away from being here and now,
and the greater the conflict within.

Only when you let go of whatever is in the future
do you create an opening
for the unfolding experience of the timeless, limitless Now.

Karma is unresolved interaction with reality
as it is revealed in the present.
It is the universal law of cause and effect.
Cause and effect are intimately entwined.
Yet they are separated by space and time.

Every moment is the experience of an effect whose cause lies in the past.
That which was caused in the past reveals its effect in the present.
If you react, you reinforce the karmic seeds of the past.
If you embrace the moment, you burn the karmic seeds in the present.

Caught in reaction, you return to the limitations of the past.
In the present, you are in the field of unlimited possibilities.
To be free from the bondage of karma is to live the experience of every moment,
consciously and unconditionally.

When part of you is absent from where you are,
You are separated in time and space.
You are divided.
Part of you is here, anxious to get there.
You are in continual conflict between here and there.

You live with the promise of the future, while in perpetual reaction to the past and recreating it in the present.
The unresolved past returns as reaction in the present.
If you perceive the present to be the problem, how would you be happy when you arrive in the future?
The moment you get there, you are back here.

When you are focused on the future,
You are blind to what is present.
You prevent yourself from seeing what is, in favor of what you want,
You create conflict with Reality.
To resolve conflict, you must enter it.

By being present, there is no part of you that is separated.
Instead of deriving seductive satisfaction from dreams and desires,
you unconditionally embrace and experience what is present.
Conditions are of the mind, the present manifests beyond the mind.

Acceptance of what is,
frees you from fear and insecurity.
You are no longer driven by desires to control.

This moment needs no adjustment, improvement or modification to
what is,
what is within, or
what is without.
This is an absolutely perfect moment.

When you realize this, you enter the deep state of stillness from where you receive
all the guidance and protection you will ever need.

Acknowledge this glorious moment, the most sacred that has ever existed.
This is a unique moment that will never again be the same.
Only when you realize its perfection does communion begin.

Everything we know originates from our direct experience

through the heart.
All that we learned as children came from being in the beginner's mind,
which is always fully present in the feeling center.

When we become excessively cerebral, our feeling center starves.
Uprooted from the nourishing ground of feeling,
thoughts become abstract and empty,
distorting our ability to feel.
Communication between the body and mind deteriorates.
This is the body-mind split, the root of all human suffering.

Staying in the beginner's mind connects us to the pure direct experience of feeling
without distortion.
The feeling center unites us with the reality of what is present.

Whatever you do to feel good,
you must feel good while you are doing it.
The secret of the good life is not the good you want at the end,
but the good feeling you carry in your heart.
When good feelings are lived experientially, they become part of you.

The good results you desire live in your mind.
The good feeling you have pervades your whole being.
Goals are in the future; feeling is in the present.

Achievements do not change the way you have conditioned yourself.
Conditioning does not stop at the end.
Suffering that has become a part of you continues.
What you have achieved is overshadowed by what you have become.

Those who live for the future, live in their mind, bound by time.
Sensitivity to how they are in the present is diminished.
Whatever feeling dominates
is what you have practiced all along the way.

Unconscious forces fragment your attention.

Your energy becomes scattered and without focus.

The mind wanders and becomes unproductive and self-destructive.

The mind is stolen in two ways—through external and internal disturbances.

External disturbance is short-lived.

Internal disturbance is long-lived and is the function of the unconscious process.

It shows up as reaction.

It is "reactivated" action.

It is the past reoccurring in the present.

External disturbance continues through your internal reactions.

It lives on and on through reaction.

Bring your scattered attention back to what you are doing at the present moment.

This is the first stage of conscious awareness.

All doing that leads to a destination
lives in the dimension of time and space.

Time-bound concepts prevent you from being in the present.

To enter this sacred spaceless space, you need no time and no effort.
All you need is be willing to experience life's unfolding, moment to moment.

The present moment is so narrow,
there exists no space to accommodate the opposites of for or against.

The present is the domain of grace.
It showers freely upon the one who remains
in the state of open receptivity to what is.

Part of us lives in past memories.
Part of us lives in future dreams.
This leaves very little room to live in the present,
where life is happening.

Being in the present,
there remains nothing to reject,

nothing to accept.
nothing to change,
nothing to manage,
nothing to control.

In the present,
You move from the separative field of duality to the unified state of being.
You are left with nothing to do.
Everything is as it is.

In the present,
you awaken from the dream of separateness
into the reality of oneness.

We are accustomed to basing achievement
on success or failure.
Everything we do to achieve success invariably creates its opposite.
The path to God is the path of grace, not the path of achievement.

We are a product of grace in the present,
not of achievement in the future.

As long as we are caught
in good and bad,
right and wrong,
success and failure,
we cannot step onto the path to God.

Carefully examine what it is that you desire.

Where does it come from?

Why does it come with such intensity?

Why can't you escape it?

Your desire won't leave you alone even when you want to leave it alone.

None of your desires are independent.

They are your unresolved past history.

Every desire is designed to compensate for what you feel is missing in your life.

You continually seek compensation through desires.

When you live in the past or the future,

what happens in your unconsciousness,

any decision you make,

any philosophy you cling to about life,

any conclusions you come to about things in the world,

how your relationships are,

what you want,

what you want to avoid,

all your likes and dislikes,

will inevitably show up.

When you learn to let go of your choices for or against,

you let go of the need for compensation.

The solution to seeking endless compensation
is to live in the present,
the narrow space between the past and the future.

In reality, there is no future.
It is only a modified version of the past.
In the present, there is nothing of the past and nothing of the future.

To live in this space is very difficult.
There is no room for ego there.
Ego cannot be accommodated in such a narrow space.
This is why it is called the razor's edge.

Reasoning is not a means of solving problems.

It is a means of coping with distrust and insecurity.

Solving problems mentally leads to divisiveness—a win-lose situation.

Dropping into deep relaxation,

trust solves problems automatically—a win-win solution.

Trust is essential for one who walks the spiritual path.

Faith allows you to live effortlessly and freely.

Let the essence of truth and faith work for you.

Remain at home with what is.

The secret of life

is the ability to enter into the present moment.
As you learn to live through experiences with childlike openness,
grace will begin to flow through you.

When, like a child, you experience life with emptiness and wonder,
then life itself,
with all its mystery,
will fulfill your deepest longings.

The present is the sacred shrine of the divine.

The future cannot survive in the present; neither can the past.

The present is omnipresent.

It has no beginning

It has no end.

It has no past.

It has no future.

It is whole, in and of itself.

Only when you are in unity with the whole

can you enter the holy temple of the present.

When you are total and undivided, you are instantly in the Now.

The life you have lost to the past,
you can only take back in the Now.
The life you live in the memory of the past,
is re-lived as reaction to the present.

The past exists nowhere other than your memory
Tethered with attachment and fears.

The past lives as memory in the present.
The future lives as potential in the present.
Both the past and the future are played out in the present.
The past is present in the Now.
The future is potent in the Now.

When the present is shadowed by memories of the past
or eclipsed by anxieties of the future,
the potency of the present is diminished.

The lessons of the past are in the present.
The possibilities of the future are in the present.
The present, stolen by the past or the future, is impotent.
All that matters is Now.

Part III
Loving Unconditionally

Our experience of the world,
people and relationships, is the result of our perceptions.
We associate our experiences through a filter of expectation.
What we encounter is not a direct experience of reality,
but a distorted version we call "my personal experience."
If we compare our experience of this moment
with our unresolved impressions of the past,
they surface as either "I love it" or "I hate it."

But when we embrace all experiences with equanimity,
they become an experience of unconditional love.

Happiness is what we most want,
investing all our resources to attain it.
Yet it is a rare event when we can maintain happiness
for more than a transitory moment.

Ordinary happiness is an experience of our conditions.
Our pursuit of it is prompted by our partial perception of reality.
True happiness—an unexplained abiding joy—happens only
when we are in harmony with the wholeness of reality as it is.

I have no friends; I have no enemies.

I have only attractions and repulsions; likes and dislikes.
When they are externalized, I call them friends or enemies.

Those whom I call friends are extensions of my attractions.
Those whom I call enemies are extensions of my repulsions.
Attractions and repulsions are actually my own attributes
revealed through my friends and my enemies.

My attractions, I call "love."
My repulsions, I call "fear."
Both my loves and my fears are played out in the relationships
of my friends and my enemies.

When my values change, my friends change.
Those whom I call friends are part of my passing attractions.
My repulsions are nothing more than attractions worn out by time.
My enemies are nothing but changing attractions in time.

In the beginning, my lover is my friend.
In the end, the same friend may turn into my enemy.

When the attraction of marriage diminishes in time, it becomes divorce.
The shift from attraction to repulsion is a change that takes place in time.
In reality, there are no friends or enemies, marriages or divorces.
There are only shifting time-bound attractions and repulsions.

Attractions come from neither another nor from outside oneself.
They are projections of myself onto the objects of my changing likes and dislikes.
There is only one enemy: the self-image that identifies with my likes and dislikes.
It becomes the victim of belief in friends and enemies, marriages and divorces.

So I do not blame the one who reveals and represents my dislikes.
I do not need to control or change the other.
I have no need to either hold onto my friends or resist my enemies.
All I need do is let go of my attractions and repulsions.
When I let go of what I dislike, I embrace the enemy unconditionally.

Yoga is the ultimate marriage of Shiva and Shakti that has no opposites.
Yoga is the experience of union within,
where attractions and repulsions disappear into Oneness.
Enemies and friends alike are embraced with compassion and unconditional love.

Everyone is looking for love with another.
What we are really looking for is the inborn evolutionary urge to merge,
to unite, to become One.

In attempting to find love outside,
we often suffer the opposite of love—disillusioned romance.
The failed romance generates anger, jealousy, fear, revenge and hurt.

When we attempt to find love outside,
we ignore the real source of love within.
Instead of giving,
we demand,
we have expectations,
we grow dependant on the other.
This creates division of love.

While the resources of love can be many,
the true source of love is oneness.
When conflict resolves, what emerges is the integrated "you."
The undivided whole that you are is born.
Union happens only when you give love unconditionally,
and connect with the source of unlimited unity within.

We explore our human potential outside ourselves.
We explore our divine potential from within.

Happiness that comes from outside is potentially a source of unhappiness.
The dream of romantic love and the nightmare of divorce live together.
When romance is actualized, divorce remains dormant as a potential.

The search for love from outside is essentially a search for wholeness.
Attraction to another is an attempt to fill the void missing in yourself.
It is a quest for the experience of ecstasy and unity.
As long as the object of love remains outside of you,
it will also be a source of fear.

Opening your heart is like falling in love.

When you are in love, you don't have to practice concentration.

You don't have to create visualizations.

You don't have to attend self-help seminars.

It just happens.

When your heart opens, you don't have to practice anything.

You don't have to perform yoga postures or breathing exercises.

Everything happens by itself.

This is the power of love for God.

With an open heart comes spontaneous chanting and dancing.

With chanting comes breathing

and with dancing comes yoga that is a dancing, breathing yoga,

alive with its own vitality.

You dance your way to God.

When you dance and sing with so much love and ecstasy,

the formal practice of postures or meditation is not an issue.

It simply happens.

You don't have to learn anything.

It all emerges from within.

Love brings integration spontaneously and effortlessly.

Everything that you want, that you want to create,

floods automatically into your life.

Love is a sacred power that dwells in
the cave of your heart.

It surrounds you, protects you and feeds you.

It spreads its wings and soars into the limitless sky.

It arrives before you get there.

It is your sacred messenger.

It is your guardian angel.

It is invisibly apparent to everyone who comes into its presence.

It is so radiant it penetrates everything it encounters,

and infuses it with its purity.

Love is not just for the chosen few.

It is abundantly available to all those who are open, willing and present.

The soul reveals itself through the body.

It longs for unconditional love and happiness.

This urge to merge, to be loved unconditionally, is an evolutionary impulse.

When this impulse works through our unconscious forces,

we see both our problems and our solutions as being controlled from the outside.

When the same impulse becomes conscious,

our attention is turned inward

and we realize that what we long for is right here, right now.

Only by going to a place deep inside yourself ....

is the soul's longing fulfilled.

Love is not an action you can perform.
When the heart opens, you are whole and undivided.
It is an effortless happening.

Love is an awakening that springs from the core of your being.
It penetrates the darkness as a beam of radiant light.
It is the state of your being.
It is the very breath of your soul.

Just as your life is sustained by breath,
Your soul is sustained by love.

There are many virtues.
Among them, love is the highest.

By lifting a flower of love,
a whole garland of virtues comes to you.

Where there is love, there is happiness, peace and bliss.
Where there is love, there is God.

Love sustains itself through continuous nurturance.

When you love yourself, it is mirrored in your love for others.

What you hold within is what is reflected from the world around you.

If you demand love, it disappears.

As you give love, it grows.

When your heart is awakened,

the purity of that love emanates its fragrance like a blossoming flower.

Unconditional love comes with ultimate flexibility.

It accommodates everything that life presents at any given time.

The contagious power of love attracts the highest in life.

Undivided love is both whole and holy.

You are a traveler on the path of love,
where there is perpetual opening…
with nowhere to go
and nowhere to arrive.
There is just the journey,
in which every step is infused with bliss and fulfillment.

Know that life is a celebration.
Each moment is reason for joy.
Knock at the door of love and be willing to enter.
Once you pass through, you will never be the same.

The source of love is within you.

Whatever you are willing to put into life
is precisely what you are ready to receive.

When you give love unconditionally,
what comes through you is pure grace.

Love embraces both ups and downs,
both the spiritual and the mundane,
providing continual opportunities for it to grow.

As enticing and attractive as your dreams may appear,
learn to anchor your love to the earth.
Give it feet to walk and wings to fly.
As long as love is unconditional, it matters not whether it walks or flies.
It fulfills all functions, both practical and spiritual.

When grounded in purity,
love soars beyond all dreams and reveals reality.

When love awakens from dreams,
it makes no demands.
It gives itself unconditionally.
When it moves from the heart to the head,
the spirit of love is lost.
Create a temple in your heart for love to reside.

It is the presence of love that makes one out of two.
The undivided whole is the nature of universal love.
All personal interests and selfish attitudes fall apart in its presence.

Unconditional love brings all conflict into union and bliss.
Such love is the life and breath of the soul.
Self-abiding is the shrine of the soul.

The secret of love is that the moment you demand it,
it disappears and conflict appears.
An intimate relationship is impossible
when you demand that which you are unable to deliver.

When you are ready to give without expectation,
conflict disappears and love reappears.
Love gives you only what you are willing to give to it.

Instead of asking for love, be loving.
Instead of waiting to be understood, be understanding.
Instead of looking for attention, be attentive.
Instead of wanting to be loved, be giving.

Giving instead of demanding heals separation.
Love will make you whole again.

Love is not an exchange.
It does not wait for a return.
Anything you expect from love turns it into a marketplace.

When we expect love to come from the other, it invariably fails.
The key that unlocks your heart is hidden in the heart of the other.

Only when your unconditional love succeeds in opening the heart of another,
do you find the key that unlocks your own heart.

There is no direct way to get love.

It emerges from giving and expecting nothing in return.

When love comes to you from unconditional giving,

You receive it as divine Grace.

Part IV
From Becoming to Being

What is becoming?

Becoming is driven by the perception of deficiency.

It focuses on accomplishment rather than upon the process.

It remains ever unfulfilled and wanting

It is separative consciousness,

leaving the doer suffering from isolation and loneliness.

What is being?

Being is the state of complete integration...

when your body, mind, heart and spirit are in harmony.

It is total alignment of what you are doing,

what you are thinking and

what you are feeling.

It is absorption in Oneness.

How do you move from Becoming to Being?

By learning to be the Witness,

By living in the present moment,

By loving unconditionally.

By being in an integrated state of wholeness...

When what you are is also who you are.

In search of the divine, we go everywhere.
We go to the places of pilgrimage,
visit temples,
follow many paths,
and disciplines,
but ignore our bodies.

Our body is the temple of God.
It is the most sacred place of pilgrimage you will ever come to.
It is the dwelling place of the divine.

When yoga is performed with inward focus and meditative awareness,
the physical body is infused and impregnated by the spirit.
It becomes the womb for the divine to manifest.

In postures, be in communion with your body.

In pranayama, be in nurturance of your hara.

In dealing with others, be caring and compassionate.

In relationships, learn to give before you demand.

In interaction with yourself, be the Witness.

In chanting, connect with your heart.

In meditation, go deep into your soul.

Surrender means letting go
of who you are not,
so that who you really are,
may emerge.

You are not what you think.
You are not what you believe.
You are not what you like or dislike.
They are merely self-concepts,
filters of the self-image that veil the hidden Self.

The purpose of the Witness is learning to surrender.

You are not exercising your personal beliefs.

You are exorcising them.

Exercising means taking action according to your reaction,

by running away or denying.

When you do neither, you let go of the habitual patterns that hold you back.

What you are you exorcising is your self-image.

You have spent your entire lifetime expending energy to sustain this image,

with all of its angers, fears, personal biases, likes and dislikes.

These self-concepts have no reality whatsoever.

No one does anything to you,

other than what you do to yourself.

Ultimately what comes to you is you.

Surrendering re-connects you with your true Self.

It is the means of moving from becoming to being.

You have a body,
a mind,

emotions,

sensations,

opinions,

choices and feelings,

but you are none of them.

"I am" exists in ultimate purity.

Anything that you add to it is an adopted extension to the self-image.

Whatever you have, you can change, you can modify.

You can either approve or disapprove of it,

but "I am" remains changeless.

The changeless among all change is who you are.

In the witness, you are the observer of all changes.

The moment you return to the witness and live there,

all objects changing in space and time lose their power.

"I am" is the highest state of being.

Regardless of how many sins you have committed,
no matter how long you have lived with guilt, shame and self-rejection,
you can be instantly released from them all
when you return to the seat of witness and realize that "I am."

The more often you return to "I am"
with nothing to add and nothing to take away,
you disengage from the karma of your past.
Witness is the only elixir that can instantly purify all that is of this world.

You may choose to undo karma as an exercise.

To create karma, you have walked around a pillar with a rope 100 times,
To undo it, you must walk counterclockwise 100 times to unwind it.

The Witness does not require an unwinding process.
Instead, the Witness creates the fire of tapas.
It burns the rope of karma rather than unwinds it.

When you are in the Witness,
you are in the pure state of "I am" and your being emerges.

What I think I feel is not always correct

because what I think is not always correct.

Most of what I feel is created in my mind.

Even though I want to feel one way,

I go on thinking the other way.

Not knowing how strongly my feelings are shaped by my thoughts,

I go on avoiding what I feel and creating what I resist.

What I feel about me is not me.

What I think about me is not me.

I am more than what I feel or think.

I am an ever-expanding circle of the mystique of consciousness.

I am a center without circumference.

The flow of energy in my body is a sacred dance.
I observe the miracle of wisdom my body demonstrates.
I adore it.
I love it.
My love and appreciation grow many fold.

My body is not something I exploit, violate or ignore,
but a living temple of God.
When I enter my body through the door of consciousness,
Nothing in the field of my awareness remains the same.

Only in the state of choiceless awareness
do the scattered forces of body, mind, heart and spirit
come together to function in harmony.

When you are total and undivided,
your internal disturbances and distractions,
indecision and impatience,
struggles and desires,
disappear into the light of unity.

Stress that exists in the conflict of becoming
dissolve in the integrated state of being.

That which observes all our thoughts,
words, emotions and actions is awareness.

Awareness is an extension of our being.
It is empty of thoughts, images and symbols.
It lives in deep silence.
It is not bound by time or space.

Awareness has nowhere to go,
It needs no time and no space to exist.
It is omnipresent.
It embraces everyone and everything unconditionally.

Awareness has no highs and lows.
It is a steady unwavering presence.
There is nothing you can add to it to make more.
There is nothing you can take away from it to make it less.

It is self-fulfilling, self-luminous.
It is not the effect or the cause.
It is the source of all that exists.
It is our own individual soul,
the spark of the supreme soul.
When you live in meditative awareness,
you are in communion with God.

When the conflicting forces of duality
resolve into harmony,
it is the embrace of the lover and the beloved.
It is the orgasmic dance of Shiva and Shakti.
It is the union of energy and consciousness.

In it, you are transported from personalized duality
to the impersonal dimension of unity.
It is the merging of the separated drop of the persona
into the cosmic ocean.
The individual drop disappears and assumes immortal consciousness.

Yoga postures create the dance of Shiva and Shakti.
They are the vehicles that propel the spirit toward oneness.

Asanas performed with meditative awareness
embody the authentic meaning of yoga.
The posture that carries spirit is the posture of consciousness.

Yoga, love and consciousness share a deep connection.

All three lead to the experience of integration.
If you elect to practice one, the other two come with it.
You cannot practice one to the exclusion of the others.

If you are in love, it will invariably lead you toward the unity that consciousness is.
If you practice consciousness, you will experience the union that love is.
If you practice yoga, both love and consciousness will naturally manifest.

Love is the invisible force that produces visible miracles.
In essence, the climax of sexual union is the same as spiritual union.
But sexual union is fleeting.
It provides only a glimpse of the ultimate possibility for perpetual union.
This glimpse is the basis for our evolutionary yearning
that continuously draws us toward the urge to merge.

This experience of union, where all separations dissolve,
is so ecstatic, you long to return to it again and again.
Merging into oneness, the separative walls of the ego crumble.
You disappear into oneness; you are no one.
This is the experience of: When I am not, God is.

There is no climax in divine love
until the separateness of male and female dissolves into oneness.

There is no consciousness
until unity is seen in multiplicity.

There is no yoga
until multiplicity merges into unity.

When you awaken the power of the Witness,
crisis becomes the fuel for transformation.
It is in this sacred space—the altar of your soul—that metamorphosis happens.

In the domain of grace,
your visualizations are realized,
your visions are actualized, and
your deepest prayers are answered.

All transitions are turning points.
They are painful but empowering.
They are opportunities to regain the freedom to be in your Source.

The turning point comes to take something away from you.
Although it may appear to be a loss,
it has come to return to you that which you always wanted from the outside.
Transitions invite you to turn within.

Trust in this process.
Let go of what is going.
Create space for what is coming.
Do not depend on reasoning that prevents you
from moving toward the self-sustaining source within.

Trust is not an act of submission or indifference.
It sees the invisible in the absence of reason.
It is your wakeful surrender to what is present.

Being present perpetually reveals the mystery of life.
The mystic is the one who allows the mystery to be.
He lives in awe of the mystery rather than seeking relief in explanations.
Trust reveals the truth, not by reason but by surrender.
Truth is that which unites you with your true Self.

All conflicts arise when one becomes two.

All conflicts resolve when two become one.

One is the dimension of grace.

When you ask for nothing,
what comes to you is grace.

You need not seek it out.
If you are engaged in achieving it, "you" become the obstacle.
Grace is not an exchange for something you have done.

To receive grace, you need not do anything.
There is nothing that needs to be achieved or changed.
Just to "be" is grace.

The moment you judge what you receive,
- you move outside the domain of grace.

If you make it the object of your ego,
- you move outside the domain of grace.

When you claim ownership to it,
- you move outside the domain of grace.

Merging into creation is the experience of grace.

Meditation is the doorway to the state of being.
It leads you to the transformative, harmonizing and balancing
force of your inner self.

Meditation is the most powerful tool of the spirit.
It creates the opening for you to effortlessly shift

- from the survival domain to the evolutionary dimension;
- from downward and outward movement to upward and inward;
- from fragmented conflict to balanced integration.

When you enter the sacred ground of grace,
you develop a heart so unconditionally open
it embraces all opposing experiences
without choosing one against the other.

Yoga is integrative.
Ego is separative.

Separation is at the core of all human suffering and problems.

Integration is the ultimate solution.

God is oneness.
This leaves no space for anything else to exist.

God is not just the Creator, but omnipresent creation itself.
God is omnipresent throughout His creation.

God is the presence of the universal laws that are unbending and unyielding.
There exists nothing outside the unconditional presence of God.

As you harmonize the forces
of your body, mind, heart and soul,
the bliss of your being begins to manifest.
It is a magnetic force that attracts synergistic forces, people, places and events.

It spontaneously brings true joy and fulfillment,
health and happiness,
wealth and well-being,
prosperity and personal satisfaction.

Despite the fulfillment of prosperity,
you never grow dependent on what you have,
because you are inherently connected to who you are.
The glory that comes to you is not achievement motivated by ego,
but is the secondary manifestation of your primary connection to the Source.

When you are deeply rooted to your heart center,
you manifest through being,
rather than through doing and becoming,

You carry within you and around you an energy field
of unconditional love.
Its sweetness exudes from your body and from your being.

True prayer happens when you are silent...

when you go beyond the individual mind and contact the Universal Mind.

When your mind is silent. . .
the vastness of that which is behind it begins to reveal itself.

When divine power surges through you,
all the secrets of life come to light.

*The masterpiece of creation is being one
with the Creator,*
where the performer becomes the performance.
Nothing can be added; nothing can be taken away.
It is the self-fulfilling experience of the self-luminous source that you are.
You are simultaneously everywhere and nowhere.

When you enter the sanctity of stillness in motion,
you are in the timeless state of being.
That which is the source of your being is also the source of existence.
In this state, you are one with the ocean of undivided existence.

Spiritual experiences happen in
the present moment.
Both past and future have no real existence;
they live in the mental dimension of memory and projection.

All human suffering and stress
take place in the dimension of time
and disappear in the timeless state of non-doing.

When the mind returns to where your body is,
when your mind does what your body is doing,
when your mind unconditionally embraces what your body is feeling,
when your thoughts, feelings and actions move as one,
you merge into the integrative experience of union.

Yoga is the experience of moving from doing to being,
from future to the present,
from the time-bound state of body-mind
to the timeless state of the soul-being.

It is a union of opposites
where you enter the paradoxical dimension of effortless effort,
non-doing in doing and
stillness in motion.

Only in the present do you become the recipient
of the grace that flows from non-doing to being.

When released energy is drawn to the Third Eye,
the nerve channels are flooded with freed prana
sending a shower of light through every cell of your being.

In this sacred moment of the union of Shiva and Shakti,
there is an explosion of nameless joy.
The mind is drained of all thoughts and images.
The empty mind becomes an invitation
for all of existence to converge its exquisite beauty, bounty and blessings.

In the moment of climax,
the union of sun and moon,
Ha and Tha,
male and female,
the walls of separation and duality crumble.
The empty mind merges into oneness, bathing in divine bliss.

In this emptiness is the culmination of yoga,
where the rivers of energies from all parts of our being
flow into oceanic unity.

Shiva and Shakti are timeless transcendent lovers.

Both reside in our body and our being.
They operate as supreme consciousness and primal energy.

Shiva and Shakti are intrinsically bound.
Together, they are present throughout creation.

For creation to come into existence,
unity consciousness divides itself into the polarity of male and female,
of Shiva and Shakti.
Primal energy manifests in multitudes of forms.
Manifest Shakti operates through polarity, time and space.

Shiva consciousness, operates beyond polarity.
It is a dimension of the soul;
It is alpha and omega,
without beginning and without end.
There is nothing that is before it,
There is nothing that is beyond it;
Therefore it is omnipresent and beyond time and space.

Through the cycles of evolution,
Shiva consciousness manifests into the individualized sense of "I am."
It is born with the urge to merge with its source of unity.
In human beings, the Shiva and Shakti that live in unconsciousness
possess the divine potential to be consciously reunited.
This is returning to the Source.

The merging of the performer into the performance
is the emergence of an entirely new entity.
The one who was performing has disappeared into being.

The manifestation of the being occurs beyond the body-mind dimension.
It is the melting of separative consciousness
into the oceanic love of the universe.
It is the integrated state where movements merge into meditative oneness.
It is the domain of the spirit where miracles happen.

This is yoga.
This is the experience of ecstatic unity.
It is the paradigm shift where all that we have failed to achieve
through doing happens in non-doing.
It is moving from becoming to being, from multiplicity to unity.
In the state of unity, there is no inside or outside to the being.

When being manifests in the timeless ecstasy and unity of yoga,
it exudes its exquisite beauty,
showers its grace and
bestows its blessings on all those it encounters.

When you identify with your self-image,
you identify with the mask of personality.
It is an adopted self.
Your self-image works not for you, but against the real Self that you are.

The adopted self is like a cloud that constantly changes
while the sky itself remains changeless.
The self-image has power only because we identify with it as "myself."
It has no existence other than the belief that:
"I am my thoughts,"
"I am my emotions,"
"I am my perceptions,"
"I am my opinions."

You have thoughts, emotions, perceptions and opinions,
but you are not your thoughts and emotions.
They change all the time.
They take your life energy and convert it into destructive actions and feelings.
They are clouds that conceal the sky.
To identify with them is to deceive yourself.
The real you is as changeless and limitless as the sky.

When you realize that your self-image steals your life away,
you are glad to let it go.
To let go of it is a special occasion.
Every time you catch yourself reacting,
take delight in letting go and know that nothing can disturb the joy in your heart.
Nothing can disturb the peace.
Nothing can destroy the love that you are.

And that is a celebration of life.

The result of your doing is called reward.

Grace is not the result of doing, but is the experience of the present.

Non-doing transports you to the state of being,

where you become totally engaged in what you are doing while you are doing it.

You move beyond all sense of time, effort and concern with the end result.

You become so absorbed in the present that your doing becomes your being.

The shimmering presence of the being

that is dimensionless and timeless is everywhere.
The moment you are present, you can perceive it.

The entity that is empty and full,
everywhere and nowhere,
everything and nothing,
spreads its ineffable presence, splendor and glory.

In deep silence, the Presence reveals itself.
There is no room for the doer.
The disillusioned doer does everything to enter this sacred space
but everything he does prevents him from entering.
Any thought of doing, improving, changing or enhancing Its glory
eliminates any chance of being in Its enchanted space.
When the moment is subjected to judgment, the Presence disappears.
The moment is perfect and only silence knows it well.

Out of the ashes of the silent doer arises the phoenix.
The actions of the silent doer are virgin actions.
The silent doer has no personal motives
That are in conflict with impersonal reality.
The action that arises from the doer's motiveless presence
manifests into actionless action.
It leaves no debit on his karma ledger.
Behold the beauty of action, where the actor has disappeared.
All that is left is a miracle.

About the Author

Yogi Amrit Desai is widely recognized as one of the leading authorities on yoga and holistic living. As a teacher, his special gift is his unique ability to present profound essential yogic wisdom as a practical method anyone can adopt. His very presence radiates the inner warmth, divine joy and spiritual energy that are the outward expressions of awakened consciousness.

Yogi Desai's spiritual odyssey began at sixteen in Gujarat, a rural western state in India. At that time, his Guru, Sri Swami Kripalvanandji recognized that the young Amrit possessed special gifts as a spiritual teacher. As a result of his Kundalini awakening in 1970, Yogi Desai directly realized the unity within all life and the divine essence within each of us. This experience became the basis of the work he called Kripalu Yoga, Meditation in Motion, in honor of his Guru. In this work, he refined methodologies that shattered the current notions of yoga as a physical discipline and opened the way for participants to embark on a path of self-discovery and enlightenment through the practice of yoga and meditation.

Immigrating to the U.S. in 1960 to study at the Philadelphia College of Art, he soon realized his true calling lay in the teachings of yoga. He founded a Yoga Ashram in Sumneytown, PA, that later grew into the Kripalu Center for Yoga and Health, the largest center of its kind in North America. For the next 20 years he continued developing this yoga system. Today, his methodology is taught and practiced by thousands of people around the world.

Yogi Desai is neither a philosopher nor a psychologist. He represents a mystic, Tantric tradition, imparting energetic experience through direct transmission. He is a Master whose presence creates a palpable energetic field where synergy transports one to a state of consciousness, stillness, peace and tranquility.

LaVergne, TN USA
15 March 2010
175928LV00002BA/3/P